# YELLOW

By Patricia M. Stockland
Illustrated by Julia Woolf

Content Consultant
Susan Kesselring, MA
Literacy Educator and Preschool Director

magic
wagon

(COLORS)

**visit us at www.abdopublishing.com**

Published by Magic Wagon, a division of the ABDO Publishing Group, 8000 West 78th Street, Edina, Minnesota 55439. Copyright © 2009 by Abdo Consulting Group, Inc. International copyrights reserved in all countries. All rights reserved. No part of this book may be reproduced in any form without written permission from the publisher.

Looking Glass Library™ is a trademark and logo of Magic Wagon.

Printed in the United States.

Text by Patricia M. Stockland
Illustrations by Julia Woolf
Edited by Jill Sherman
Interior layout and design by Nicole Brecke
Cover Design by Nicole Brecke

Library of Congress Cataloging-in-Publication Data

Stockland, Patricia M.
  Yellow / by Patricia M. Stockland ; illustrated by Julia Woolf.
      p. cm. — (Colors)
  ISBN 978-1-60270-260-8
  1. Yellow—Juvenile literature. 2. Color—Juvenile literature. I. Woolf, Julia, ill. II. Title.
  QC495.5.S776 2009
  535.6—dc22
                        2008001606

I wave good-bye to the bus driver.

The school bus is yellow.

Grandpa hangs up my raincoat.

My raincoat is yellow.

I eat a banana.

The banana peel is yellow.

We feel the warm sun.

The sun is yellow.

Grandpa feeds the ducklings.

The ducklings are yellow.

12

Grandpa counts the chicks.

The chicks are yellow.

I put eggs in my basket.

The basket is yellow.

We pick lemons for a pie.

The lemons are yellow.

I pick bright flowers for Grandpa.

The flowers are yellow.

Grandpa ties a ribbon around the pot.

The ribbon is yellow.

# What Is Yellow?

There are three primary colors: red, blue, and yellow. These colors combine to create other colors. You cannot make the color yellow by mixing other colors. You can make yellow darker or lighter by adding black or white.

**Primary Colors**

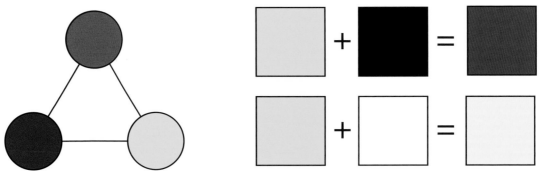

Some colors seem cool. Others seem warm. What colors remind you of a warm fire? What about a cool lake? What yellow things did you see in the story? Does yellow seem warm or cool to you? Yellow is a warm color!

# Words to Know

**banana**—a type of fruit that is curved and yellow.

**bright**—having a lot of color; a bright object stands out and can be seen easily.

**lemon**—a type of fruit that has a sour taste.

**peel**—the outer covering of a fruit.

**ribbon**—a long, thin piece of cloth used to tie things.

# Web Sites

To learn more about the color yellow, visit ABDO Publishing Company on the World Wide Web at **www.abdopublishing.com**. Web sites about the colors are featured on our Book Links page. These links are routinely monitored and updated to provide the most current information available.